$\mathcal{B}$ALLET
for Beginners

Marie-Laure Medova

Sterling Publishing Co., Inc.
New York

To my parents, my teachers, Madame Ludmilla Tcherina, and to my professional students.

Translated by Fay Greenbaum. English edition edited by Isabel Stein.

The French original of this work was published with the support of the Regional Center of Letters of Midi-Pyrénées. With the participation of: Alwa, Anne-Lise, Anne-Rose, Aurélie, Géraldine, Laetitia, Nicolas, Virginie.
Artistic direction and layout: Jean Biret-Chaussat. We wish to thank maison Vicard, which kindly lent the students' outfits.

Photo Credits: Page 6, 105 and 109 (top), Erich Lessing/Magnum. Page 7, Ballet-théâtre Joseph Russillo. Page 96, Courrault/Enguerrand. Page 104, J. P. Daudier/Explorer. Page 108, page 109 (bottom) Jacques Moatti/Explorer. Page 107, Explorer archives. The photographs of Marie-Laure Medova's class (Académie de dance classique, 18–18 bis, rue Agathoise, Toulouse) are by Gérard Dupuy.

Library of Congress Cataloging-in-Publication Data

Medova, Marie-Laure.
   [Danse classique. English]
   Ballet for beginners / by Marie-Laure Medova.
     p. cm.
   Includes index.
   ISBN 0-8069-3877-3
   1. Ballet dancing.   2. Ballet.   I. Title.
GV1787.M37513 1995
792.8—dc20

95-9224
CIP

10 9 8 7 6 5 4 3 2

First paperback edition published in 1997 by
Sterling Publishing Company, Inc.
387 Park Avenue South, New York, N.Y. 10016
First published by Editions MILAN, Toulouse, France
under the title *Danse Classique*
© 1989 by Editions Milan
English translation © 1995 by Sterling Publishing Co., Inc.
Distributed in Canada by Sterling Publishing
℅ Canadian Manda Group, One Atlantic Avenue, Suite 105
Toronto, Ontario, Canada M6K 3E7
Distributed in Great Britain and Europe by Cassell PLC
Wellington House, 125 Strand, London WC2R 0BB, England
Distributed in Australia by Capricorn Link (Australia) Pty Ltd.
P.O. Box 6651, Baulkham Hills, Business Centre, NSW 2153, Australia
Printed in Hong Kong
All rights reserved

Sterling ISBN 0-8069-3876-5 Trade
           0-8069-3877-3 Paper

Contents

She is Coppelia, the Sugar Plum Fairy or Sleeping Beauty; she is so beautiful that when you see her on stage or on television, you dream of dancing like her or becoming her partner. . . .

To see her move, light and smiling, it seems natural to leap and slide and pirouette like her, but you know well enough that it takes a lot of work to do these so easily. So, it's decided; you're going to work too! You'll sign up at a dance school. But which one? How do you choose the teacher who will suit you? And what are you going to learn there? This book introduces you to the basics of classic ballet, explains how a class is structured, and gives you all the necessary advice to begin calmly.

Your dance school will offer you exciting activities, not always without pain. Accomplishing what your teacher asks of you will require great attention, personal discipline, and effort. Your teacher will show you the correct posture, gestures, and movements and will correct you until your work is perfect. There is so much to learn, from the basic positions to *battements*, *sauts*, *entrechats*, and combinations of steps.*

To better understand and more easily memorize the movements you are learning, study the photos in this book: they were taken

4

*French terms are used in the ballet classroom, and in our book. See the list of ballet terms at the back of the book for explanations of French terms and a pronunciation guide—*Editor*.

during an actual dance class. Each exercise is illustrated by photographs, with commentaries by Marie-Laure Medova. She is a former principal dancer and also is a teacher; her students number in the hundreds, with several principal dancers among them.

As you progress, if you have moments of doubt, if you're afraid you've forgotten some exercises, return to the instructions in this book for a little review. And if later on, you want to interrupt your ballet school studies without totally relaxing your discipline, your home teacher will be nearby in this book.

Happily, dance is not just work. First and foremost, it is a joy and your way to enter into the magical world of ballet. Did you know that the first ballets worthy of the name were created in the court of the kings of France and that, all over the world, ballet steps are called by their French names? Do you know when dancers first started dancing *sur les pointes* (on toe) and wearing tutus? And all those famous ballets, *Giselle*, *The Nutcracker*, *Coppélia*, *The Firebird*—who created them? This book will introduce you to the history of ballet, from its noble origins in royal spectacles to the boldness of modern dance, visiting the romantic and classic ballets on the way.

Although it had far-off beginnings, ballet is very much alive today, but it is a closed world. Through wonderful photos, you'll step into the mysterious world of backstage. As the dance school is the training ground for that magical place known as the stage, you probably are asking yourself how a student goes from classroom exercises to a public performance. This book will tell you how a ballet is prepared and will introduce you to the work of the choreographer, the technicians, and the designers.

In this book, you have both a technical consultant and a guide to the world of dance. What are you waiting for? Let's dance!

The grace and
lightness of
classic ballet.

Dance Today

On television and in the movies
you often may have the chance to
see dances: in ballets, modern
dances, musical comedies, variety
shows. . . . And you undoubtedly
ask yourself questions: what kind of
training is needed for these different kinds of dance? How can I find
my way among all these different
styles? Here is some information
that will let you compare ballet
and contemporary dance.

CLASSIC BALLET OR MODERN DANCE?

Here are the principal characteristics of these two disciplines. It's up to you to decide which best corresponds to your temperament. Each of them can bring you great satisfaction, but don't forget that even an excellent modern dancer cannot perform classic dance if he or she hasn't received classic ballet training. Classic dance, on the other hand, will give you an irreplaceable foundation; if, later on, you don't wish to perform in that medium, you will be able to adapt yourself to any modern style.

CLASSIC BALLET

- This is a well-defined discipline, taught the same way all over the world. It is based on two great concepts: *turnout*, that is, that the legs and feet must be turned outward, and *the five positions*, from which all steps start and end. These two concepts have been followed since the creation of the Royal Academy of Dance, founded by King Louis XIV of France.

- In the tradition of royal ballets, the most important thing is to find movements and steps that are graceful, noble, and elegant. The body itself must conform to this idea of beauty; a harmonious way of holding the head, a long neck, a slender waist, and good proportions are desirable. Training, which aims at molding the body, must, if possible, start when the student is very young.

- The pursuit of lightness has driven dancers to rise and leap higher and higher. Women raise and lighten themselves by going up on toe.

- A classic ballet tells a story with characters in costume. Tutu and toe shoes are the standard costume of the classical dancer.

MODERN DANCE

- Different styles each correspond to a particular training, which goes more deeply into certain aspects of dance: contraction and release, a sense of balance, movement through space, breathing. . . .
  Always seeking to grow, contemporary dance continues to create new styles and new techniques.

- Contemporary dance tries to express modern life. It is not fundamentally searching for beauty and can also show ugliness, violence, sensuality. . . . There is no defined idea of beauty for the body, but the body must be strong and supple enough to perform movements that are sometimes acrobatic.

- Elevation has less importance. On the contrary, dancers can bend down, fall, or move along the floor, depending on what feelings they wish to express.

- Often the dance does not really have a story, but rather an atmosphere that expresses ideas and feelings. Dancers may wear a skin-tight leotard, giving the impression of nudity, or everyday clothes, or fantasy costumes. Shoes are not necessary; people often dance barefoot.

Starting Out

AT WHAT AGE SHOULD I BEGIN?
Before age 8, children's bones are too soft for the demanding technical exercises of ballet, so it's not a good idea to start before then, although you may enjoy preballet classes of movement and rhythm. It's up to the teacher to judge if you are ready for the discipline of ballet classes. It is possible to start later, at age 10 or 12, and still have a great career. To find out if you really want to study ballet, you can ask to attend a dance class as an observer. Afterwards you can make up your mind whether to sign up or not.

THE QUALITY OF INSTRUCTION
The age at which you begin is not really important, but it is essential to make a

good start. Whether you begin at age 8 or 10, you are very young and your body is very malleable, which means it can be shaped easily. If you form bad habits in the beginning, you will keep them for a long time and, even if you try very hard, it is difficult to correct them. So choose your teacher well! If you can, find out about the school where you would like to enroll: how long has it been in existence, who are the teachers, have they been teaching a long time, are they professional dancers themselves, have their students become professional dancers?

STRUCTURE OF A DANCE CLASS

A dance class lasts about an hour. First, you warm up; that is, you stretch and loosen your muscles and prepare them for more important efforts. Very young dancers begin with floor exercises, which are easier than work at the *barre* (bar). Once you have a little experience, you start the class at the *barre*.

The first exercises at the *barre* let you warm up your joints by doing *pliés* [plee-ayz´], or bends. Then, progressively, you exercise your entire leg, using the *barre* to help find your balance more easily. Next are exercises in the center of the room. You continue to exercise your legs to acquire sureness of movement, but here it is a little more difficult: you no longer have the help of the *barre* and must find your balance on your own.

Through work in the center of the room, you learn to use your arms gracefully and naturally and to move them from one position to another.

In the last part of the class, you learn to do arabesques, jumps, pirouettes, *enchaînements* [ahn-shain-mahn'], or combinations of linked steps, and series.

Throughout class, the teacher moves around. She will correct the position of one student and give advice to another. If you have not understood an exercise well, don't be afraid to tell her. She will either demonstrate again or give you additional explanations to help you progress.

THE QUALITIES OF A DANCER

A dance class is a total physical workout, requiring technique, balance, and grace. To make the best use of class time from beginning to end, you must not let your attention wander; concentrate and listen to your teacher so that you can correct your mistakes.

This will not always be easy; sometimes, certain exercises will seem difficult to you. You probably will have difficulty in carrying your body properly: head straight, shoulders relaxed, stomach and buttocks pulled in. This happens to everyone at some time. But don't be discouraged, and above all, do not doubt yourself; even the biggest stars have had these difficulties. Don't make too much of them, and don't force yourself to do work

Your body is malleable; choose your teacher well.

that is too hard for you. In dance, you must seek out balance in your spirit as well as in your body. In the beginning, you probably will take one or two classes a week; don't even think of cutting! Only regular participation and persistence will allow you to progress. Professional dancers take class every day.

11

A place that quickly becomes familiar. The *barre* helps you find your balance; the mirror helps you correct your positions; the wooden floor gives under your feet.

THE DANCE STUDIO

You'll get into the habit of coming to this room quickly and you'll end up knowing it very well. It is specially set up to help you work. The floor is made of wood or is covered with linoleum. It permits you to move and land softly after you jump. (Dancing on a hard floor can injure you.)

The walls are covered with mirrors. This is very practical to see if your hair is neat, but it isn't there for that reason. Watching yourself in the mirror is essential to correct bad placement.

Along the length of one wall, there are two *barres* to give you support for certain exercises. Depending on your height and the exercise, you can use either the top or the bottom one. Of course, you'll be doing all your exercises to music, since rhythm is the foundation of dance. You might have a pianist to play the music, or it might be played on a tape recorder.

The dressing room, where you change your clothes before and after class, is the ideal place to talk with your friends, but silence is required during class.

12

YOUR DANCE CLASS OUTFIT

Choose clothes that are snug enough to let the teacher see clearly whether your placement is correct. On the other hand, they should not be too tight; you have to feel comfortable in them.

In general, girls wear a leotard and tights. At the beginning of class, since your body is not yet warmed up, you can add leg warmers and a short sweater. You'll take them off once you're warmed up. Your hair mustn't get in your way and should also contribute to giving you a clean silhouette. If it's long, put it up in a bun or put it up in braids around your head: these hairstyles expose the nape of the neck and give your head a pretty line. Add a headband to keep wisps of hair in place. If you hair is shoulder length, put it up with hairpins and a headband. Even short hair—whether boys' or girls'—can be restrained with a headband.

Boys' dress traditionally is sober: black tights and a white T-shirt. Manufacturers offer many more imaginative and colorful outfits for boys as well as girls, however. Depending on the school you go to, your dress will be plain or imaginative. You will perspire a lot during a class: don't forget to wash out your outfit each time you use it. Try to take care of your dance things: since they're made of stretchable fabrics, you could wear them two years in a row, unless they have holes or are torn!

The clothes you wear during class are the same ones currently in use in many exercise classes and are not expensive,

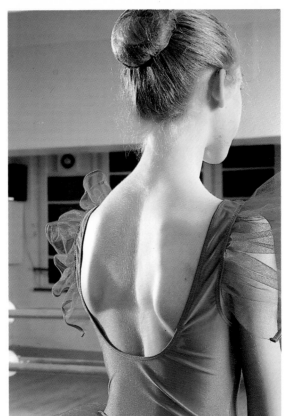

Hair tied in a bun gives a pretty shape to your head.

13

Ballet slippers, toe shoes, leotard, and tutu: the basic girls' outfit.

A white
tutu and
toe shoes:
the classic
dress for
performance.

but many schools have a big night: a gala at the end of the term or the year! For that special time, you need special clothes. The teacher will decide on each person's costume. For the girls, it could be the famous tutu of the ballerinas—a skirt made of several layers of gathered tulle or other fabric. It can be short, mid-length, or long, depending on the type of performance. Mothers frequently help to prepare for gala time, and often create very original costumes.

BALLET SLIPPERS

Boys wear black or white ballet slippers of thin leather, held on the foot by an elastic. Girls have pink shoes of leather or satin. They start out wearing ballet slippers and don't use toe shoes (*chaussons de points*) until the teacher decides that their ankles, back, and other supporting muscles and bones are strong enough to take this kind of exercise. Like the boys' slippers, girls' ballet slippers can be held in place on the foot by an elastic.

Shoes are sold without the elastic. It's up to you to sew it on. ▼

Older girls may prefer satin ribbons tied around the ankle.

Ballet shoes are expensive as they are made by hand. So as not to ruin them, don't put them on until just before class and don't let them get wet. You can wash the ribbons, however.

Toe shoes are reinforced in the toe according to secret methods jealously guarded by every craftsman. It is necessary to change them often, as the toe stiffening becomes soft. A professional dancer can use as many as ten pairs of toe shoes a month!

HOW DO YOU SEW ON THE RIBBONS?

Shoes are sold without ribbons or elastic. Dancers have to sew them on themselves. You'll need a pink satin ribbon about ½ to ¾ inch wide (1 to 2 cm) and about 39 inches (1 m) long. Fold the heel of the slipper back towards the toes; sew the ends of the ribbon to the inside of the slipper on each side of the stiffening (see photo). Then pull the ribbon taut and cut it in the middle. And there you have it! If you can't sew yet, ask someone who can to show you how to do it.

HOW TO TIE THE RIBBONS

You will very quickly learn to tie the ribbons correctly: neither too tight nor too loose, so that they will support you without bothering you. First cross the two ribbons in front of your foot and bring them back behind your heel. Cross

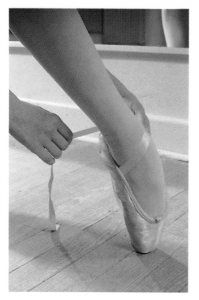

The ribbons are first crossed at the front of your foot.

Then they are crossed behind the heel and the ends are brought forward.

After having been crossed a second time in front of the foot, the ribbons are tied behind the ankle.

the ribbons behind your heel and bring them back around to the front. Cross the ribbons in front, just below the first crossing. Take them back behind your heel and make a double knot. The ribbon ends should be invisible; tuck them well in under the ribbons.

IF YOU PRACTICE AT HOME

It is essential to take certain precautions. Don't try to dance if you feel tired or if your muscles ache after a dance or gymnastics class. Warm up slowly, gradually. Don't try to rush ahead without it. Wear warm and comfortable clothes. As in the dance studio, you need a smooth wooden or linoleum floor. Don't

ever dance on a hard surface.

Always be aware of your posture and correct it as often as necessary. Think also of breathing, as your teacher has shown you.

It is normal for you to sometimes find what you are learning difficult or strange, but with a little time it will become habit, and you will be more comfortable with the new developments. Practicing at home is a good chance to see whether you understood the previous class.

When you use this book as a reminder, read the commentary carefully before trying to reproduce the movements shown in the photographs. If there is something you don't understand, don't hesitate to ask your teacher.

The Classic Dance Lesson

So here we are, ready to enter that magical place: the dance studio! Remember, here neatness is required: no hair flying loose or twisted tights!

At the very beginning, you'll learn to walk gracefully, run lightly, and listen to the music, its beat and nuances. That is really a lot, as dance is based on rhythm and tempo.

A classic dance lesson is given in two sections: one at the *barre* and one in the center of the floor. For newcomers, class will include some floor exercises known as a floor *barre* (*barre à terre*), and then a small *barre* exercise, very simplified. The lesson will finish up in the middle of the floor with simple exercises that teach balance. *Barre* work is essential because it allows us to warm up and loosen up progressively. This is also where you will learn to "place" yourself; in other words, to hold your body, head, arms and legs in proper alignment to each other. In general,

it takes two years of beginner's class in order to achieve a good placement and move up to a more advanced class. In order to ease you into work at the *barre*, you will do floor exercises in the beginning. Your teacher will show you how to make each movement and will correct your position and help you to perform certain movements—stretches, for example.

The Five Positions

Even in your first classes, you should learn about the famous law of turnout. This fundamental principle of classic dance has been followed for four centuries. Turnout, quite simply, is a position you get by rotating the legs outward at the hip joint. Your knees and feet follow the same direction, of course. What is its purpose? To avoid blocking the hip joint at a certain height, which would otherwise occur when you raise your leg. Thanks to turnout, your legs have greater freedom of movement. As you progress, you

▶

will gradually improve your turnout, so don't force your body to do more than it is ready to do.

The five positions were defined by the great dancing masters of the 17th century, notably by Pierre Beauchamp, the ballet master of Louis XIV, king of France. It is for this reason that French is used all over the world to name the classic dance steps. Without the five positions, you couldn't learn a single movement. In fact, almost all classic dance steps start and end in one of the five positions. Their purpose: to give the dancer maximum balance. Each position of the feet has a corresponding position of the arms.*

---

*Note: The arm positions shown in this book are numbered by the French school system of numbering. In your dance class, they may be given a different number or name if your class follows the Italian (Cecchetti) or Vaganova (Russian) or R.A.D. method of teaching, or some other method—*Editor*.

First position

In French, it's *première position* [prehm-yair′ paw-zee-syawn′]. *Feet:* The heels are together, legs stretched straight. Turn your toes outward to form a straight line.

Arms: In the beginning position, place your arms along the sides of your body. Slightly supported, they should form a curve. Keeping this curve, raise your arms above your waist. Your hands should be held between the level of your waist and the level of your chest.

21

Second position

In French, it's *seconde position* [seh-gohnd' paw-zee-syawn']. *Feet:* Separate them sideways, about 1½ feet apart (46 cm). Make sure they are well turned out.

Arms: Open your arms to the side, rounding them slightly; your elbows should be at a slightly lower level than your shoulders.

Third position

In French, it's *troisième position* [trwah-zyem' paw-zee-syawn']. *Feet:* Put the heel of your right foot against the middle of your left foot.

Arms: Bring your right arm up in a semicircle for *troisième en haute* [trwah-zyem' en-noht']; the other arm stays in second position.

Fourth position

In French, it's *quatrième position* [kah-tree-ehm′ paw-zee-syawn′]. Slide your right foot forward so that it is parallel to your left foot, with about 12 inches (30 cm) between them.

Arms: Place your right arm overhead in a vertical position: your left arm is in first position.

Fifth position

In French, it's *cinquième position* [san-kyem′ paw-zee-syawn′]. Place your right foot close up in front of your left; the toes of each foot should touch the heel of the other.

Arms: The two arms, overhead in a vertical position, form a round shape that frees the neck and shoulders. There is a small space between the hands. This position is *cinquième en haute* [san-kyem′ on-noht′] or *bras en couronne* [brah-zahn koo-rohn′]—arms in a crown shape.

Floor Exercises

Floor exercises allow you to get that famous turnout necessary for classic dance. Exercising your dorsal (back) and abdominal muscles also will give you better back and stomach muscle development.

1 Sit on the floor with legs bent. Soles of the feet are facing each other, toes are touching. Separate and raise your heels slightly. Be sure to keep your back perfectly straight! Stretch your head upwards and let your elbows rest on the floor.

2 From this position, raise the right leg, keeping it perfectly straight and turned out.

4 Flex and then point your toes, alternately. Take care! Your leg should always be well stretched to the side. Come back to the starting position and make the same movements with the other leg.

5 You can complete this exercise as shown in the photo—hands holding ankles; soles of the feet touching, which gives you a point of support for straightening your back and lowering your knees toward the floor. This is how we work on turnout at the hips.

Working on turnout at the hips

3 Now move your straight leg out to the side.

27

28

1 Lie on your back, arms to the side, legs together and straightened.

Developing the back and stomach muscles

2 Leaving that position, sit up by bending both legs, with toes on the floor, heels lifted, arms rounded before you, and back perfectly straight. Very slowly, go back down to the floor to the starting position. This exercise should be repeated several times.

1 Lie on the floor, legs straight, with one crossed over the other, making sure to point your toes.

3 Bring the extended leg out to the side without touching the floor. The back and pelvis should remain flat against the floor.

2 Raise one leg in an extended position; it should be perfectly straight.

Raising the legs and turning out the hips

This exercise should be done in one slow movement. To exercise both legs, all you have to do is repeat the exercise with the other leg.

4 Come back to the starting point, brushing the straightened leg against the floor.

31

5 At the end of the series of exercises, raise yourself up to a sitting position, arms rounded over your head (in fifth position), legs straight, to perfect the work on back and stomach posture.

1 **2** Starting from the last position of the previous exercise, these two photos show you several movements to lengthen the lumbar spine, that is, to make the lower (or lumbar) part of the spine more limber.

32

3 **4** Still in the starting position (seated, legs straight, arms rounded over the head), you can complete these movements by stretching one arm to the side. Your head should turn to follow the direction of your arm.

Making the spine limber

5 Switch from one side to the other, each time passing through the *bras en couronne* (fifth position). All of this is done to the rhythm of the music.

Turning out the hip joints: more exercises

1 Take the position of the first exercise: seated, with legs bent, soles of feet facing, with toes touching. Raise and lower your knees to the sides, in order to gently and progressively get a greater turnout of the hips.

34

2 Then straighten your legs, toes pointed, and separate your legs as much as possible in the direction of the floor. Bend them again and come back to the starting position.

1 Keep your legs as spread apart as possible and place your hands *en couronne*, keeping your back straight.

2 Lower your left arm while rotating your chest to the left.

Lateral chest stretches

35

3 Extend your chest over your left leg. Your right arm should be parallel to your left leg. The left arm is kept in second position. Gently come back to your starting position. Repeat the exercise on the right side.

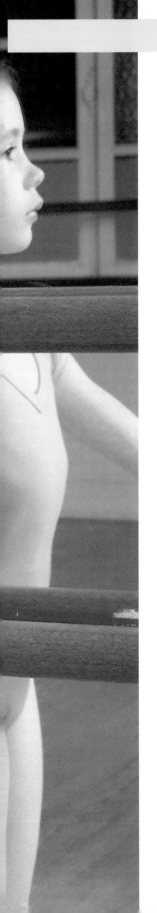

The *Barre*

Like the floor exercises, work at the *barre* is meant to warm up the muscles and perfect your turnout. It is also preparation for exercises in the middle of the room and for the steps you will dance in ballets later on.

The *barre* [bahr] is a wooden support that lets you find your balance more easily. It is fastened to the wall of the practice room at about hip height. It also helps you to hold yourself correctly and have good placement. All the *barre* exercises should be done on one side and then on the other in order to work both sides of your body equally.

37

The length of time for *barre* exercises depends on the level of training of the students, but should never exceed half an hour. Why? Because a good *barre* will warm up the different muscle groups, without tiring the dancer, who will next be facing exercises in the center of the room.

Exercises at the *barre* follow a well-established order. All *barre* exercises must start with *pliés*, because they stretch all the muscles of the legs and are preparation for the exercises that follow. They also make turnout easier.

There are two types of *pliés*: in *demi-pliés* (half bends), the knees are bent halfway. This movement stretches the heel tendons in particular, as heels are still securely on the floor. In *grands pliés* (big bends), the knees are completely bent.

Pliés should be done in each of the five positions. Take note: you must be neither too close nor too far from the *barre*, and the hand resting on the *barre* should be slightly ahead of your body.

◀ **1** *Pliés* [plee-ayz′] are leg bends. Stand in profile to the *barre*, with your feet and your free arm in first position.

2 Carry the arm from first to second position, that is, the arm opened out to the side with the elbow supported.
▼

3 Do a *demi-plié* [d'mee-plee-ay′]. The heels are together and remain on the floor, the knees are bent halfway (*demi* means "half").
▼

40

Pliés in first position

4 Here is a *grand plié* [grahn plee-ay′]. The knees are completely bent. The free arm moves down to the starting position. The heels come off the floor.

5 The legs slowly straighten and come back through *demi-plié*, to their original straightened position. The arm rises to first position, and then opens to second when you change position.

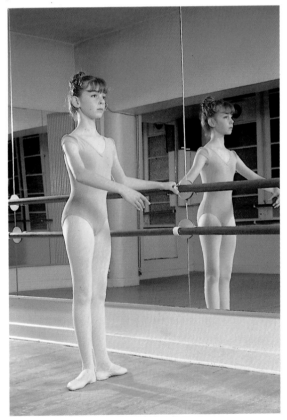

41

1　Here is what we call a *dégagé pointé à la seconde* [day-gah-zhay′ pwan-tay à la seh-gohnd′]: the free foot is pointed in second. It allows you to move from first to second position.

2　Second position. The feet are separated and the heels are well into the floor.

3　Go from a *demi-plié* to a *grand plié*. The heels stay on the floor. The free arm goes down to the starting position and goes back up to first position. Careful! In the *plié*, the knees should be directly over the feet in the same vertical plane.

Pliés in second position

43

4 Come back up, legs straightened, with your free arm in second position and your heels turned forward.

5 On *demi-pointe* [d'mee-pwant'], which means "on the balls of the feet," find your balance, letting go of the *barre* or holding on.

1 In order not to lose your balance during the following *plié*, you must be careful to distribute your body weight between your legs.

2 For the *demi-plié*, open your knees.

Pliés in fourth position

45

3 For the *grand plié*, your chest should be perfectly vertical, your legs well opened and your heels always turned out.

4 Do a *dégagé en quatrième pointée devant* [day-gah-zhay′ on kah-tree-ehm′ pwan-tay′ dih-vahn′], a *dégagé* in fourth position with your foot pointed in front, which will let you move on to fifth position.

1 The legs are straight and the free arm is held out.

2 *Demi-plié*.

4 Come up gently, passing as always through a *demi-plié*, legs straightened, free arm in first position.

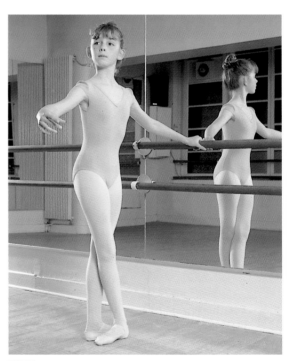

5 The free arm opens out to second position. The head turns in the direction of the arm.

Pliés in fifth position

3 *Grand plié.*

6 Find your balance with both your arms - placed *en couronne*.

There you are, you've done the exercises based on *pliés*! Well, almost! All you have to do now is turn around with the other side towards the *barre* and start again on the other side. How do you expect to form a well-balanced body if you don't exercise both sides equally?

47

The second series of exercises will allow you to review all of the exercises that dancers do at the *barre*.

1 *Dégagé* the straight leg in front, pointed to fourth position. The shoulders are thrown back. The pointed toes should not leave the floor. So that the free foot will always be turned out, you should have the feeling that you are pushing your heel forward.

2 The feet are placed flat on the floor in a fourth position *plié*. The weight of the body rests between the legs. The knees are turned out.

4 Bend both legs in second position, keeping the knees well turned out. The feet remain flat against the floor.

5 Now *dégagé* the working leg to fourth position back (*quatrième derrière*), keeping the knee turned out. Don't move your hips!

Dégagés, pliés, tendus

[day-gah-zhay′, plee-ay′, tahn-diu]

3 *Dégagé* the extended leg to second position.

6 Finally, *plié* in fourth position back (*qua-trième derrière*), supporting your ankles well.

49

1 The pointed foot should come off the floor. *Dégagé* in fourth position in front (*quatrième devant*) to *demi-hauteur*.

2 Here is the same movement in second position (*à la seconde*).

50

3 . . . and here it is in fourth position behind (*quatrième derrière*).

Dégagés à la demi-hauteur

or *petits battements jetés*

[day-gah-zhay′ a la d'mee-oh-tuhr′; or p'teet baht-mahn′ zheh-tay′]

Demi-hauteur **(literally, half-height) indicates the leg is at a 45-degree angle to the body.**

Ronds de jambe à terre pointés

[rohn dih zhahnb a tair pwan-tay′]

In this exercise, the foot makes a half-circle as it slides along the floor. This is an excellent exercise for limbering up the hip joint and improving your turnout. It is perfect for beginners. *A terre pointé* means the toe remains on the ground and is pointed.

51

1 Face the *barre* with feet in first position, back straight, ankles supported, knees straight.

2 Keeping your body weight over the supporting leg, point the free foot, with leg well stretched, to fourth position in front (*quatrième devant*) to start the *rond de jambe en dehors* [ahn duh-aur′], which means you are circling from the front to the back.

Ronds de jambe
à terre pointés

3 Move your foot along the floor to second position. The toe remains pointed and on the ground.

4 Continue around to fourth position behind (*quatri-ème derrière*), with the pointed toe still on the floor.

5 Finally, come back to the starting position. This exercise is then done *en dedans* [ahn dih-dahn′], that is, starting the exercise at the back and circling to the front. Don't forget to repeat the exercise with the other leg also.

Battements frappés

or *battements sur le cou-de-pied*

[baht-mahn' frah-pay' or baht-mahn' siur lih koo-dih-pee-ay']

In this exercise, you bring your free heel alternately in front of and behind your other ankle, which doesn't move. Performed quickly, this exercise allows you to develop briskness. The *cou-de-pied* is the area above the ankle and below the calf muscle, which is where your heel goes in this exercise.

1 The *battement frappé* is done here in fourth position in front (*quatrième devant*). You can also do it in second position, and in fourth position behind (*quatrième derrière*). Raise the straightened leg to *demi-hauteur*.

2 Then bend the working leg, bringing the free foot in front of the ankle of the supporting leg.

53

54

Grands ronds de jambe pointés

[grahn rohn dih zhanb′ pwan-tay′]

Here, big *ronds de jambe* are done in the air with pointed toe. This exercise is done to very slow music called *adage* [ah-dahzh′]. This word, which comes from the Italian *adagio*, also means "gently."

1 Raise the free leg to fourth position in front (*quatrième devant*), while opening your arm out to second position. Don't forget to keep your hips level throughout the exercise.

2 Then, while your body weight stays over the supporting leg, the free leg, still in the air, moves to second position.

3 Then it moves to fourth position behind (*quatrième derrière*). In this way it makes a circular motion, an *arabesque ouverte* (open arabesque). The free arm is *croisé devant* (crossed in front of the body). Then the free foot is lowered while pointed to fourth position behind to repeat the exercise in the other direction.

4 Foot pointed in fourth position behind (*quatrième derrière*). The side of the big toe should rest lightly on the floor. Arm in sixth position.

5 The same movement, but this time the arms are in third position.

55

Arabesque and second position

The arabesque is also an *adage* movement, which should be performed very gently.

1 The back should be stretched to the maximum, the head upright. The supporting leg, *relevé* (raised) on *demi-pointe*, should be quite stretched. The free leg continues the line of the back.

56

2 Second position *à la hauteur*, which means that the free leg is raised to waist level. The supporting leg is perfectly straight. The other leg is stretched and turned outward. The back is perfectly straight. From this position, do your *ronds de jambe en l'air à la seconde* (in the air in second position), from front to back (*en dehors*), and from back to front (*en dedans*).

3 The same exercise with the arm in third position.

1 In this position, with the supporting leg straightened, you can make little beats above your ankle, either stopping or continuously, by very quickly passing the heel of the free foot in front of and then in back of the supporting ankle.

Petits battements sur le cou-de-pied

or *petits battements serrés*

[p'tee baht-mahn′ siur lih koo-dih-pee-ay′ or p'tee baht-mahn′ seh-ray′]

57

2 **3** Finish with your hands on the *barre*, with a balance exercise. The supporting foot is raised on toe or *demi-pointe*; the free foot is "*retiré*" [drawn up]* at the knee.

Take care! The knee of the working leg should stay open, the thigh stays still. This exercise is preparation for *petite batterie à croisement*, a movement during which the legs and feet beat against and cross each other.

*Note: In the French system, this is called *raccourci* [shortened]—Translator.

Balancing in *retiré à la seconde**

[rih-tih-ray′ ah lah seh-gohnd′]

When your working leg is drawn up and the thigh is opened out to second position, with the toes of the working foot pointing to the supporting knee, it is in *retiré à la seconde.*

58

1 Keep the same position as in the previous exercise, but with your profile to the *barre*, arm in third position. Try to find your balance.

2 Then let go of the *barre*, placing your arms *en couronne.*

*Note: In the French system, this is called *raccourci à la seconde*—Translator.

Pied dans la main

[pee-ay dahn la man']

Pied dans la main means "foot in hand."

1 Bring your free leg up to *retiré* at the knee
(retiré au genou).

2 *Plié* the supporting leg.

59

3 Take the heel of your free foot in your hand and stretch
your leg in front of you, keeping your leg turned out.

4 **5** Pull your leg around to second position without raising your hip.

6 Let go of your heel, placing your arm in second position.
Your leg should stay in place and be perfectly straight.

1 **2** With feet in first position, stretch your torso forward, keeping your back flat.

3 **4** Try to touch your straightened knees with your nose ... then bring yourself back up, keeping your back very flat.

Stretches with the back to the *barre* for beginners

5 Come back to the starting position.

6 Once there, find your balance on *demi-pointe*, with arms in first position.

1 Chest placement in fourth position front, and head inclined.

2 From this position you can bend your chest forward or arch backward.

3 Second position facing the *barre*. The teacher should help you with shoulder placement.

4 From this position you can bend your body alternately to each side, keeping it parallel to the leg.

5 In fourth position behind (*quatrième derrière*), with the help of your teacher, check the placement of your back and leg.

Pied sur la barre means "foot on the *barre*." This is the last loosening and stretching movement, which usually concludes the *barre* exercises and precedes the split.

Pied sur la barre

[pee-ay′ siur la bahr]

6 After you have been corrected, you should be aware of the position of your body in space on your own.

7 Here is second position facing the *barre*.

8 The series concludes with a *demi-plié* in second position.

63

1 The split.

2 The split with arms in third position.

Grand écart

[grahn tay-kar′]

The split

This exercise ends the *barre* work. Spread your legs in such a way that the entire length of both legs touches the floor.

3 Finally, loosen up with a split in second position (facing front).

65

In the Middle of the Room

After the *barre* exercises, you will move to the middle of the studio where you have no support. Now you can only count on yourself for balance! Just as at the *barre*, the exercises in the middle of the room follow a progression. First you have to exercise the essential parts of the body in order to progress to small combinations. Redoing certain exercises without the support of the *barre* will develop your muscular strength and your balance, and will allow you, little by little, to go on to movements that require a more sustained effort.

In the middle of the room, you will learn the steps that are essential in preparing a ballet. The movements studied there can be found in most classic dance combinations.

The work focuses on the *port de bras* [por dih brah'], the way you hold your arms. The work the arms do is very important in classic dance. In a ballet, the arm and hand gestures often replace words. Learning to move your arms and legs gracefully and naturally requires training. Before starting, you should make sure that your posture is correct. The muscles of your arms should be supple, the wrists and elbows supported, the fingers gracefully extended.

1 2 *Port de bras en fondu** [ahn fohn-diu']: the supporting leg, which here is in front, is in a deep *plié*. The back leg is extended with the foot flat on the floor.

3 4 *Port de bras:* here is one of the numerous variations of the classic *port de bras*.

5 Foot pointed in fourth position in front (*quatrième devant*), supporting leg in *plié*, arms in sixth position.

68

*Literally, while sinking down—*Editor.

Grand plié in first position

[grahn plee-ay]

Now it's time to do this exercise, which you learned in the first part of class, without the help of the *barre*.

69

1 Start with legs straight.

3 Come back up through a *demi-plié*.

2 Pass through a *demi-plié*, keeping your heels on the floor as long as possible, to get to a *grand plié*.

4 Straighten your legs, finishing the exercise with a *relevé* on *demi-pointe*.

The *pas de bourrée* (*bourrée* step) is always done in ¾ time. (A *bourrée* is an old French dance.) In classic dance, there are several *pas de bourrée*. Here is one of them.

1 Stand in the center of the room in fifth position, with right foot behind and arms in starting position.

3 Bend the right leg with the foot in *demi-pointe* on the floor; the left leg is also bent.

2 Bend both legs and raise the arms to first position.

4 Go up on *demi-pointes* with both feet, and straighten your legs.

The *pas de bourrée*

[pah dih boo-ray′]

71

5 Staying on *demi-pointes*, move the front leg aside into second position.

6 Close up the other leg in front in a *demi-plié*.

7 To finish the *pas de bourrée*, straighten both legs and place your arms in the starting position.

Everyone knows what a *glissade* is. You move along the level of the floor, sliding your foot to the right or to the left. But why "*en descendant*"? This is an expression used in the European theatre, where the stage is always raked.* "To go down" (*descendre*) means to go towards the audience, and the opposite, *remonter*, means "to move towards the back of the stage." We say, for example: *glissade en descendant, petits dégagés en remontant.* In order to succeed at the *glissade*, do it slowly at first. Once you feel at ease with it, you can do it more quickly.

2 Bend both legs, with arms in first position.

3 *Dégagé* your left leg to second position with your foot pointed on the floor.

4 Quickly move to second position with both feet flat.

Note: A raked stage is sloped so that it is lower at the front and higher at the back. This gives the audience a better view of the whole stage. Almost all European stages are raked. In the United States, most stages are flat because the house (where the audience sits) is sloped, so that people in the back rows can see past the people sitting in front of them more easily—*Translator*.

Glissade en descendant

[glee-sahd' ahn dih-sahn-dahn']

1 Get in your starting position: in fifth position with the left foot behind.

5 Bend the left leg and point the right foot on the ground in second position.

6 Move the right foot closed in front, sliding it across the floor.

7 Finish your *glissade* by straightening both legs, with the arms in the starting position.

73

1 Stand in fifth position, with right leg in front and arms in sixth position.

2 Raise the left leg, bent at the knee (in *retiré*), and bend the right leg, with foot still on the floor.

 3 Jump while bringing up both legs, the knees well opened, toes pointed down.

4 Land on the bent left leg, the right remaining bent at knee height.

The *saut de chat**

[soh dih shah']

Saut de chat means "cat jump." It is a jump that usually is done several times in a row, while moving to the side.

5 Place the right foot in front in fifth position.

6 Finish the *saut de chat* by straightening both legs.

75

Note: In the Russian and Italian schools this step is known as the *pas de chat* (cat step)—*Translator*.

  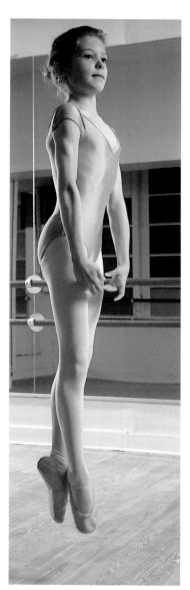

1 Stand in fifth position, with arms in the starting position.

3 Jump, keeping both legs quite straight, the feet pressed against one another, toes pointed down.

2 Bend both legs.

The *soubresaut*

[soo-brih-soh']

The *soubresaut* is a sudden leap straight upward and forward.

4 Land lightly, bending both legs.

5 Finish the *soubresaut* by straightening both legs.

Of all the dance movements, the pirouette is one of the most difficult to do. Doing a pirouette means making a complete turn around yourself, balanced on one leg, like a spinning top. The head plays a big role; you mustn't turn it at exactly the same time as the body. In fact, it should remain facing front as long as possible, but arrive at the end of the pirouette before the body!

1 Stand on your straightened supporting leg in *demi-pointe*. The free leg is bent, the knee well turned out. Your teacher will help you become aware of your balance: she will position and watch your back as you should hold it at the moment of the pirouette.

3 Bend both legs, sinking your heels well into the floor, so that you can push off into your pirouette.

4 The pirouette is completed.

78

2 Prepare for the pirouette in fourth position, legs straightened.

The pirouette

The pirouette is practiced on _demi-pointe_ for a long time, in order to do it well on toe. To stay balanced, dancers should fix their eyes on an imaginary spot on the wall, or on their own eyes in the mirror.

5 Pass your free foot behind your other knee, before putting it down in fifth, in a _demi-plié._

6 Finally, straighten both your legs.

Point Work

Almost everyone has tried out a few dance steps on the tips of the toes. In French, it's called *sur les pointes* [siur lay pwant']. To resemble those graceful ballerinas who seem to fly as they skim so lightly, hardly touching the stage, what a dream!

The reality, however, is a little different: dancers usually go up on *pointes* (toe) around 12 years of age. Only the teacher can determine whether your ankles are well placed enough and sturdy enough to begin to practice *pointes* work. You absolutely must not go on toe as long as you do not have enough strength in your ankles and without the direction of a qualified teacher, because you can injure your bones, which are still developing. Your muscles must be well trained to bear your weight correctly before you go on toe, also. What distinctive feature do we see in toe shoes? In fact, they are specially reinforced at the tips. In this way, your own toes are no longer in direct contact with the floor, as they were in ballet slippers. This explains why your first pair of toe shoes gives you a feeling of complete imbalance. Before going up on toe, you must have a sturdy and well placed back, as well as ankles capable of supporting your body perfectly.

A professional dancer has to change her toe shoes often. In fact,

1 To start with, here is a slow movement, broken down at the *barre*, in second.

2 Without bending your knees, go up on *demi-pointe*.

3 Raise yourself up onto your toes, without bending your knees; keep your shoulders still and push your heels towards the *barre*.

4 Remaining on toe, keeping your feet spread apart, do a *plié* in second position.

the glue softens and the shoe loses its stiffness. You should always choose toe shoes that are a little tight. Don't forget that when you go up on toe, your foot moves down in the shoe; you can understand, therefore, why you must sew the two 20-inch [50 cm] ribbons very securely to the shoes, as they help to hold them on your foot.

In order to get used to your toe shoes, at first, you should do several exercises at the *barre*. This will help you place your ankles, add to their strength, and will help you control your back and find your balance.

Exercise no. 1

83

5 Stay in this position, then come down from your toes, passing through *demi-pointe*.

6 Place your heels on the floor, ankles high and the feet spread flat against the floor.

7 Straighten both legs.

8 Go back on toe and work on balance. This exercise should be repeated several times, with musical accompaniment, of course.

1 Do a *demi-plié* in first position.

2 Straighten both legs.

4 Go up on toe.

5 Come back down onto *demi-pointe*.

Exercise no. 2

3 Rise up on *demi-pointes* without bending your knees.

6 Finally, place both heels on the floor, with legs straightened. Begin the exercise again with a *demi-plié*.

85

Exercise no. 3

1 Stand in fifth position. Then do a *relevé au genou* with your free foot; your supporting foot is on toe.

86

2 *Relevé* with the free foot in *retiré au genou*; the back is facing the *barre*.

3 Finish with a *relevé* in fifth position, with your free arm in third position.

Échappés sur pointes

[ay-shah-pay′ siur pwant′]

Échappés sur pointes literally means escaping movements on toe. If by now you are fairly at ease at the ***barre***, you can try some exercises in the middle of the room.

1 Stand in starting position, legs straight, feet in fifth position.

2 Bend your legs. Bring your arms up to first position.

3 Separate the legs, going up on toe; the arms move to second position.

4 Bring your feet back to fifth, switching the forward foot. The legs are bent; heels are on the floor. In this position you can do a series of *échappés*.

87

1 In the starting position, the legs are straight, arms in sixth position.

2 Bend both legs.

4 Raise yourself on point on both feet.

5 Move the left foot, which is in front, out to second position.

Pas de bourrée

[pah dih boo-ray′]

Bourreé step

3 The right leg, which is in back, slides out to second position, and is pointed.

6 Come down from your toes, and close your right foot up in front by sliding it over the floor, with legs in *plié*.

7 Finally, straighten both legs.

89

1 In the starting position, the right foot is in front.

2 Place your arms in first position.

4 Rise up on toe; your free leg is in *retiré* at the knee. Your weight rests on the supporting leg.

5 Come back down into fifth position, bending both legs.

Relevés au genou

[rih-leh-vay' oh zhnoo']

3 Bend your legs, while moving your arms to sixth position.

6 Finish your series of *relevés* by straightening both legs.

***Relevés* with free foot at the knee**

91

Temps de pointes en descendant

[tahn dih pwant' ahn
dih-sahn-dahn']

Moving forward on point

1 Stand with legs straight, with right leg in front and arms in sixth.

2 Bend both legs.

3 Slide the right foot to fourth position, forward (*quátrième devant*); the supporting leg is bent.

4 On the right foot, go up on point, placing the left foot behind the knee.

5 Bring both feet together in fifth position, legs in *plié*.

**This movement concludes in *plié*;
you can do it several times in a row.**

The arabesque

The arabesque is very difficult to perform as it requires excellent balance. You have to balance on one leg and lift the other leg behind you. Your teacher will help you to do the arabesque.

93

From School to the Stage

You may be planning to continue to study dance and, perhaps, make it your career. This chapter gives you some information about the choices open to you, and some ideas of what a dancer's career is like.

SCHOOLING

The teaching of ballet is not uniform all over the world. In the United States, there is no central authority that sets standards of teacher training and curriculum in ballet. Teaching by the Cecchetti (Italian)

or Vaganova (Russian) methods is frequent, but other methods are also found. There are thousands of private academies that teach dance. Some teach other forms of dance such as jazz and tap, as well, but if you are serious about ballet it is best to go to a school that specializes in ballet. Classes take place after regular school hours or on Saturdays. At the end of the term or year, some schools organize a production or gala for the parents to see.

Some large cities in the U.S. have ballet companies with schools attached to them. Many students compete for a few available places, usually after they have had some previous training. In addition to ballet, the students continue to do their regular schoolwork, so ballet classes are frequently after school, in the afternoons, evenings, and on weekends. The special attraction of such a school is that it allows pupils to participate in many productions staged by the ballet company, perhaps as children at the party in *The Nutcracker*, or in a similar role. This early contact with the world of performance is a marvelous experience.

In the United Kingdom and the British Commonwealth countries, ballet is more strictly regulated and standardized. There are strong guidelines for curriculum, and examinations test the level of ability of the students. Teaching is by the Royal Academy of Dance or Cecchetti methods. As in the U.S., there are private schools, and also ballet companies with schools attached to them in large cities, which give youngsters a chance to experience life on the stage.

YOUR ENTRY INTO PROFESSIONAL LIFE

Whatever training you may have chosen, things will become series when you reach about age 16. It is time to prepare for professional life. You will learn to dance with a partner and to interpret roles. You will have new technical difficulties to overcome and you will have to learn to give style and presence to your movements.

You will also start to dance variations: in a ballet, a variation is a solo dance, a combination of movements that form an independent whole, often without any direct ties to the story. Knowing how to dance variations will enable you to audition for entry into a troupe of professional dancers.

When you are about 18 to 19 years old, you can make contact with dance companies. Find out who their directors and choreographers are and what their programs are in order to choose one where you could do diverse and interesting things. Some have schools, and taking a class will let you familiarize yourself with that company's style.

Whatever *corps de ballet* you would like to join, you will have to go through an audition—a hard test, especially psychologically, as you may feel lost among hundreds of other students applying, who are all at more or less the same technical level as you. Maybe a movement, an expression, or some details will catch the attention of the director of the company and you will be the one chosen!

YOUR CAREER

Dance, unfortunately, is a profession in which there are few job openings. A large company consists of about thirty people. A more important troupe accommodates about one hundred people. You will have to work hard to advance through the ranks. In the U.S., once you have made it into the company, you will be an apprentice. Then you will be a new dancer, then a member of the *corps de ballet*. After that, you could be a soloist and maybe, finally, a principal dancer. There are very few openings for the most important positions.

The *corps de ballet* is the large group of male and female dancers who move together onstage. They must take care to coordinate their movements so that none of them separates from the group. The soloist interprets more important roles. As for the principal dancer, it goes without saying, that she has very challenging roles.

The performance career of a dancer is

very short. Before the age of 20, it is difficult to forget technique and let your personality and expressive qualities show through. People reach their full potential at around age 25. At around age 45 for a man and 40 for a woman, or even earlier, it's necessary to give up performing! Many dancers end their careers even earlier; this is an exhausting profession, for men as well as for women. Knowing this progression from the start, you can calmly envision what you will do after you cease to perform. You may decide to be a choreographer, a teacher, actress, artistic director, ballet master, or dance critic.

HOW TO SUCCEED PROFESSIONALLY

Of course you must have good technique, but making dance your profession also requires certain personality traits. Here is a portrait of the ideal professional dancer. (Our example is a woman, but a male dancer requires the same traits.) It's up to you to decide whether you resemble her or whether you would like to resemble her.

A professional dancer has a good memory and knows how to stay in shape through healthy living and balanced meals. She drinks no alcoholic drinks, including wine. She knows that adequate nutrition is essential to develop and maintain healthy bones, muscles, and joints, and to have the strength and energy necessary for ballet. She avoids the use of tobacco, the enemy of breathing.

She is dynamic, with emotional resilience and a strong will. Even and especially when she does not have a role in a production, she must continue to work, with one or more teachers. She is aware that even if she achieves recognition, she will always have to work very hard. She is so involved with dance that she has not had time to go on to higher education, but she has a great deal of general knowledge; this is very useful when it comes to discussing contracts, defending her rights, and managing her income. It is useful for her to learn French, as the ballet uses French terms throughout the world and she may find dance opportunities in Europe. Finally, she has completed her training by learning to play a musical instrument; a dancer who doesn't know how to listen to music will never be able to dance.

Even if she is a little shy, she knows how to get on with others and make contact with choreographers and directors. She is very curious about everything happening in the world of dance and in the arts in general. She stays well informed about the artistic scene and doesn't hesitate to move in order to meet future partners. She knows that finding a role that suits her in a company where she will feel good is mostly a question of how she gets along with others.

She likes living in a community and adapts very well to the hazards of life on tour or abroad. After all, she is passionate about dance and is happy to be able to earn her living by dancing, even if it is not a profession where you earn much money.

The Dancer's Life

Staging a production is the work of a team. Here is how the activities of a French dance company are organized. (The details may vary from country to country, and from company to company.)

It is ten o'clock. All the dancers are ready for class: an hour and a half of work at the *barre* and in the center of the room, as it has been every day for years. Then rehearsal of the ballet. Whether the work is new in the company's repertoire or is a ballet that is already known, it will take about one month's work to get it in shape.

Before the performance, in the wings: nervousness, warm-up, and solitude.

Preparations before the performance: a little rosin to avoid slipping.

The artistic director supervises the rehearsal. He is the one who chose to stage this ballet, and contacted the choreographer, designers, and musicians. He gave out the roles to the dancers and guides them in their work.

The choreographer takes part in the rehearsal to make sure that the choreography he has conceived of is correctly danced. He is not always a member of the troupe; often, it does not have the means to pay him a permanent salary. When this production is ready, the choreographer will leave to work elsewhere.

You work until two p.m. and usually continue rehearsing from 3:00 to 6:00 p.m., but this afternoon calls for rest, for this evening is the final dress rehearsal, the last rehearsal before the public performance.

The "countdown" began a week ago. First there was the technical rehearsal, which provided the opportunity to finalize the practical organization of the production. The set is perfect. It consists of a cloth backdrop painted in optical illusions, plus a few props. It suggests a certain atmosphere, but leaves plenty of space for the dancers. This set, in fact, derives its importance from the lighting; the set designer carefully worked out the effect with the lighting designer. A natural-looking light gives way to a muted atmosphere and, a little later, the sunrise is suggested by red sunbeams. Sometimes the stage is brightly lit, sometimes it is steeped in shadow as a follow spot tracks the movements of the soloist in its beam

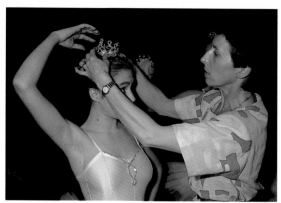

▲ Adjusting a hairdo.

of light. It is a subtle play between spotlights of different strengths, of more or less focused lenses, possibly modified by masks or colored gelatins.

If there is no orchestra, the sound engineer has checked that the sound system for the prerecorded music is working well: this means that the work of the musicians will not be badly presented, and that all spectators will be able to hear very well, whether they are near the stage or at the back of the house. The technical director checks all the details and coordinates the work of each technician.

After the technical rehearsal, there is the dress rehearsal. This is the first time that the dancers are in costume, and the wardrobe master has plenty to do to get everything ready. It is the wardrobe master who has made the costumes, following the designs of the costume designer, and will take care to wash them, repair them, and arrange them for as long as the performances run. What a problem if a costume has been mislaid! The dress rehearsal finally lets us judge the effect of everything together and is a time to correct certain details.

▲ Putting on makeup.

And this evening is the *final dress rehearsal*! It will unfold under exactly the same conditions as a public performance would.

The dancers arrive two hours before the curtain is raised. They start putting on their makeup in their dressing rooms. A layer of foundation spread over the face compensates for the intensity of the lighting. Then, with the help of pencils, the dancers accentuate their features so that their eyes and mouth can be distinguished from far back in the audience. Makeup also serves to express the traits of each character: pride and wickedness for one, gentleness and sadness for another.

101

Above, left: A final choreographic note before the final dress rehearsal.

Above, right: The final dress rehearsal unfolds under the same conditions as a public performance, including costumes and lighting.

Right: Before the performance: some warm up, others chit-chat.

Then the dancers put on their work clothes to go and gently warm up their muscles in the dance studio of the theatre. Next, they go back to their dressing rooms to finish their preparations (hairdo, finishing making up) and put on their stage costumes, with the help of dressers. Once their ballet shoes are well tied, a last look in the big mirror and there they are, ready to go down to the stage. There, before the curtain is opened, they once more rehearse some of the technically difficult parts of the ballet they are going to dance.

It's more than a quarter hour before the start of the performance. . . . The musicians take their places in the orchestra pit and tune their instruments. The stage manager calls for the lights to be turned down. In the dressing room, you can hear the music of the overture over the public address system. And the curtain goes up! The dancers think of nothing now but dancing, while the company director watches their movements. It is he who has negotiated the contracts with the dancers and musicians and who pays their salaries. He manages the troupe's budget, looks for grants, prepares tours. If this performance goes well, he'll be able to produce others. He already has some ideas. . . .

In the house, the press agent is seated among the journalists she has invited. She will have to organize interviews, collect articles that have appeared in the press, and have photos taken of the production. When the troupe goes on tour, she is the one who will contact newspapers and radio stations so that they will announce the performances in each city. The

Finally, the curtain has gone up. No one thinks of anything now except dancing.

reputation of the production and of the company rests on her.

The final dress rehearsal was perfect! The production will be a triumph, and in a few weeks the company will go on tour for several months. They will take the set, the lights, the props, the costumes. . . . Each dancer will have an individual locker to arrange clothes, makeup, and shoes.

Some members of the troupe will be a little sad to leave their families for such a long time. Dance is an exciting profession, but it requires many sacrifices. If you are a woman dancer and you marry, it is absolutely essential that your spouse share a passion for dance, even it he is not a professional dancer himself. It's important to learn about the laws and contracts that affect you, especially if you are planning to have children. Pregnancy and maternity laws and benefits vary from country to country, as do vacations and the number of weeks of paid work a dancer gets each year, which will affect your family life. In the U.S., some dancers are represented by a union, the American Guild of Musical Artists; in the UK, dancers are represented by British Actors Equity. Most dancers love the travelling life, even if they have hardly any time for sightseeing: with performances every evening until midnight; rest in the morning, then at two o'clock dance class for an hour and a half and rehearsal. In short, days and nights are very full: dance is not a profession in which you get bored!

The four virtues, characters in the *Ballet comique de la reine Louise* (1581), an early court ballet.

A SHORT HISTORY OF DANCE

In all ages and all countries, people have danced. Originally, they danced in honor of the gods. But dance was also able to dramatize concepts such as war or love, or express the joys and pains of individuals. According to legend, when Theseus got out of the labyrinth thanks to the thread given him by Ariadne, he and his companions improvised a dance that symbolized the thread running through the twists and turns of the labyrinth: this was the first farandole.

The Romans, like the Egyptians, Hebrews, and Greeks, had sacred dances, but they especially appreciated the dance as entertainment. In the Middle Ages, due to wars, disease and famine, death was constantly present. People felt they must take advantage of life, it was so short. So they danced more than ever, in churches, chateaux, and village squares.

THE BIRTH OF THE BALLET

The Renaissance, while continuing the dances of the court and the villagers, brought a more elaborate form of dance: the *ballet comique* (comic ballet), ancestor of today's ballets (*comic* means "theatrical" here). One of the first ballets was created by the Italian Balthasar de Beaujoyeulx. It was the *Ballet comique de la reine Louise*, given in 1581 at the *Palais du Louvre* (Louvre Palace) in France. The plot was taken from Homer's *Odyssey*. The queen, princes, and duchesses participated, and the music, poetry, dance, and set were all specially created to work together and tell a story. Such theatrical ballets had great success. Since the fashion was for things about ancient Greece and Rome, all the gods and mythological heroes were put on stage, some in works created by the most famous writers of their time. The great lords and the noble ladies of the court all wanted to appear in these ballets, especially as the queen and king were in them, but their talents didn't always measure up to their aims. King Louis XIV of France, noting that "several persons, however ignorant and inept they have been in this art of the dance," had joined in the ballets, founded the *Académie royale de danse* (Royal Academy of Dance) in order to "reestablish the aforesaid art in its perfection." The superintendent of this academy, Pierre Beauchamp, codified the dance and defined the five basic positions, still in use today.

In 1681, Beauchamp presented *Le Triomphe de l'amour* (*The Triumph of Love*), to the music of

Lully. In it, professional female dancers played the female roles for the first time. Up until then, female roles had been given to men or noblewomen, who were transformed into sweet young girls or desperate lovers by the masks they wore. This new idea became the rule: from then on, there were professional dancers capable of interpreting more and more complicated choreography in the salons of amateurs and on stage.

WOMEN AFFECT DANCE

In the 18th century, the French school of dance was reputed to be the best in Europe, but the ballets were very boring. A young woman named Marie Sallé tried to bring warmth and passion to the dance. She wished to make it express her emotions and to be freer, she dared to dance without a corset and without a wig or other head ornament. Her ideas were not immediately accepted at the Royal Academy in Paris, so Marie Sallé choreographed the ballet *Pygmalion* in London (1734). The ballet was a triumph, and Marie opened the way to the emancipation of female professional dancers, who, until then, had only had secondary roles. Out of modesty, they were supposed to limit their movements, while the male dancers were admired for their agility.

Another female French dancer overcame the boundaries set for women dancers. Marie Camargo, who debuted at the Paris Opera in 1726, jumped and beat out *entrechats*, steps reserved in those days for men. Despite those who found it indecent for a woman to show her ankles, she didn't hesitate to shorten her skirts so that the play of her feet could be admired.

For liberty, against the academy: this was also the idea of Jean-Georges Noverre, who in 1759 published his *Lettres sur la Danse* (*Letters on Dancing and Ballets*), revolutionary for their time. Throughout Europe, he presented ballets whose subject, stage production, and dancers' gestures were worked out like a theatrical play; everything was permitted in order to convey emotions.

La fille mal gardée (English title, *Useless Precautions* or *The Wayward Daughter*), a ballet created by Jean Dauberval, is a good illustration of the new ideas of the time. Its theme was drawn from everyday life and its heroes were simple peasants: it was 1789, on the eve of the French Revolution. This ballet is still very popular; it contains scenes full of gaiety and spirit.

THE AGE OF ROMANTICISM

Ballet was to find new life in folkloric dances, Anglo-Saxon legends, and in technique that became better and better. Two ballets from the studied elegance of the Romantic era are still frequently performed: *La Sylphide* (1832) and *Giselle* (1841). *La Sylphide* was choreographed by Filippo Taglioni for his daughter Marie, who already was a well-known dancer in Europe; she had perfected what several dancers had tried before her: she danced *sur les pointes* [siur lay pwant], or on toe. The other-worldly theme of *La Sylphide* suited the technique of toe dancing and the style of Marie Taglioni perfectly.

Marie Taglioni's great rival at the Paris Opera was Fanny Elssler, a Viennese ballerina whose style was very different. She loved gleaming costumes, folkloric dances, fiery rhythms, and pantomime. She incarnated another facet of Romanticism: an attraction to the exotic and to folklore. *Giselle*, created in 1841 for dancer Carlotta Grisi, with a score by Adolphe Adam, illustrated these two tendencies of Romantic ballet.

From then on, female dancers were to eclipse male dancers. Women became the reference point, the standard. The male dancer was only the partner, the porter who aided his partner in her flight by lifting her. No one was surprised when *Coppélia*, created in 1870, had a male role played by a female dancer in disguise.

Village dances, *Coppélia*.

THE CLASSIC BALLETS

Coppélia (score by Léo Delibes, choreography by Arthur Saint-Léon) is still popular today. It was

Patrick
Dupond and
Jean
Guizerix,
principal
dancers in a
production of
*The
Nutcracker*,
1982.

The Nutcracker was based on a famous story by Hoffmann, *The Nutcracker and the Mouse King*, in which a young girl named Clara receives a nutcracker shaped like a soldier as a Christmas present, which comes alive. She helps the nutcracker (who is really an enchanted prince) to battle an army of mice, and is rewarded by a trip to the Kingdom of Sweets. *The Nutcracker* has many children dancing in the *corps de ballet* and is frequently the first ballet many young ballet goers see. Tchaikovsky created brilliant music, perfectly in accord with the gaiety and marvel of the theme, which is still well loved today.

106

based on a fantastic tale by E.T.A. Hoffmann, about a marvelous robot.

The French ballet at this time had lost its vigor and expressiveness, but Russia, which had earlier had many guest artists, including Noverre and Saint-Léon, was to give the dance a vigor as yet unknown, as the result of the French-born Marius Petipa (1818–1910). A perfect classical technician, Marius Petipa taught Russian dancers the western tradition, while allowing them to express their strength and gaiety. To please the royalty, Petipa kept creating colorful, sparkling ballets, tinted with the exotic or with folklore. Of the fifty or so ballets Petipa created, the three that are still alive and well have scores by Tchaikovsky, which is probably no coincidence: *Swan Lake* (1877), *Sleeping Beauty* (1890), and *The Nutcracker* (1892). All three are still danced frequently today.

THE NEW SPIRIT OF THE *BALLETS RUSSES* (RUSSIAN BALLETS)

At the end of the 19th century, the French ballet was at a low point. Fortunately, some changes were occurring in the dance world that were to eventually provide it with new life.

Several American dancers brought new ideas in dance to Europe. Loïe Fuller, an American actress, triumphed at the Universal Exposition in Paris in 1900 with her dances imitating butterflies, flowers, and clouds. She waved immense veils, bathed in lights that changed color. Thus, she was one of the first to use the artistic possibilities of lighting techniques.

In the early 1900s, Isadora Duncan, an American dancer who had been studying the essentials of movement and dance, evolved a new way of dancing that stressed natural, simple, spontaneous movement. She brought her revolutionary ideas to Europe, where she was welcomed. She danced in Russia in 1904. Her dancing was seen by Russian choreographer Michel Fokine, who was experimenting with new steps, costumes, and other ideas to break ballet's blind conformity to tradition. Fokine was hired as choreographer by producer Serge Diaghilev, who in 1909 brought a company of Russian dancers, the *Ballets Russes* (Russian Ballets) to Paris.

Diaghilev brought together the best dancers, musicians, and designers of the time, including dancers Vaslav Nijinsky and Anna Pavlova; composers Igor Stravinsky, Claude Debussy, and Camille Saint-Saëns; and artists Léon Bakst, Pablo Picasso, and Natalia Gontcharova. His inspired choreographer Michel Fokine created original and innovative ballets that broke with tradition. *The Dying Swan* (1907, music by Camille Saint-Saëns), told the agony of a swan in one act. Anna Pavlova, who created the swan role, gave it in unforgettable interpretation. *The Firebird* (music by Igor Stravinsky) was based on Russian folk legends. The young Tsarevich Ivan captures a firebird and sets it free in exchange for a magical feather, which helps him deliver some young women held prisoner by an enchanter and wed the most beautiful of them. *Petrushka* (1912, music by Stravinsky) was based on a traditional puppet of the same name, and is the story of a showman and

Vaslav Nijinsky in *Schéhérazade* **(1910). A true genius of the dance who filled all who saw him with enthusiasm.**

three puppets. In the original ballet, Nijinsky played Petrushka and Enrico Cecchetti played the showman. In Fokine's *Le Spectre de la Rose* (1911, music by Carl Maria von Weber), a young girl falls asleep after a ball; the rose she is carrying falls to the ground and its spirit (originally danced by Nijinsky) starts to dance. In the morning, the young girl remembers her dream, but the rose has faded.

When Michel Fokine left the *Ballets Russes*, Nijinsky himself became the choreographer. Two ballets show his talent: *L'Après-midi d'un faune* (*The Afternoon of a Faun*) and *Le Sacre du Printemps* (*The Rite of Spring*). In *The Afternoon of a Faun* (1912, music by Claude Debussy), three nymphs meet a faun. Two run away, one stays behind. She escapes when the faun becomes too insistent, but she forgets her veil. When she comes back to get it, she finds the faun kissing the veil and leaves it to him. Nijinsky's choreography created a scandal because of its daring. In *The Rite of Spring* (1913, music by Stravinsky), a primitive tribe celebrates the arrival of spring by dancing. A young girl is offered in sacrifice; she will dance until she dies of exhaustion. The music as well as the choreography, which devised new types of dance movement, were initially greeted by a public outcry, as they were different than anything seen before.

After Nijinsky left the *Ballets Russes*, Léonide Massine choreographed some ballets, including the avant-garde *Parade* (1917). It really had no story: a magician, a young girl, some acrobats, and some tightrope walkers parade to attract an audience. The score, by Erik Satie, included the sounds of a typewriter and a car horn. Picasso's cubist costumes, although a little cumbersome for the dancers, added greatly to the ballet's originality.

Diaghilev's last choreographer was George Balanchine (originally, Balanchivadze), who earlier had been a dancer with the State Ballet in Leningrad. He revived *Le Chant du Rossignol* (*The Nightingale's Song*; music by Stravinsky, choreography by Massine), based on a Hans Christian Andersen fairy tale, for a young Englishwoman, Alicia Markova, who danced the title role, and also created original ballets: *Apollon Musagète* (1928; now known as *Apollo*), *Le Chat* (*The Cat*), and *Le Fils prodigue* (*Prodigal Son*, 1929), which revealed a new star of Russian origin: Serge Lifar.

CONTINUING THE SPIRIT OF AVANT-GARDE BALLET

When Diaghilev died in 1929, his company was disbanded, but its principal members went on to play important roles in contemporary ballet all over the world. George Balanchine, who came to the United States in 1933, founded the School of American Ballet and a series of ballet companies, the last of which was the New York City Ballet (in 1948); he helped create an American style of classic ballet. In Great Britain, Alicia Markova became a principal dancer, and Marie Rambert and Ninette de Valois each founded dance companies, which were the beginnings of what became Ballet Rambert and the Royal Ballet. In France, Serge Lifar gave new life to the Paris Opera Ballet, where he became ballet master in 1929. He helped restore the male dancer to a position of importance and created more than 50 ballets. He guided such stars as Yvette Chauviré and choreographers Janine Charrat and Roland Petit.

MODERN DANCE

We saw earlier that Loïe Fuller and Isadora Duncan were the first to free themselves from the laws of classic ballet. Other American dancers also searched out a form of personal expression in dance. Ruth St. Denis created exotic-looking dances and found inspiration in Indian dancing and culture. In 1914 she met Ted Shawn, who also was a dancer; he became her partner and husband. In 1915, they founded a school of dance, Denishawn, in Los Angeles, California. They believed that dance could be a form of religious expression and an integral part of life. Their curriculum included ballet, ethnic and folk dances, Dalcroze eurhythmics, and Delsarte exercises.

Their former students continued the growth of modern dance in the US and other countries. Among them were Martha Graham, Charles Weidman, and Doris Humphrey, who went on to establish dance companies of their own and train new generations of modern dancers and choreographers, including Graham student Merce Cunningham and Humphrey student José Limón. Independent of Denishawn were Helen Tamiris and Lester Horton.

In the 1910s, Rudolf Laban, born in Austria-Hungary, created a new form of movement, *Ausdrucktanz* (expressive dance). He founded schools in many European cities, and was very active in Germany. He also developed a system of dance notation. Mary Wigman and Kurt Jooss, his pupils, became important choreographers. In 1938, fleeing the Nazis, Laban came to England and established a dance school. Wigman pupil Hanya Holm brought German modern dance to the US.

Many other modern dancers have formed companies that have added their work to the vitality of modern dance, including Erick Hawkins, Alvin Ailey, Alwin Nikolais, Sybil Shearer, Paul Taylor, Anna Halprin, and James Waring after World War II and more recently Twyla Tharp, Laura Dean, Rudy Perez, Meredith Monk, and Yvonne Rainer in the US and Robert Cohan in England. There has been cross-fertilization between ballet and modern dance, with classically trained dancers sometimes moving to dance or choreograph for modern dance companies, and modern choreographers, such as Twyla Tharp, sometimes choreographing for mixed troupes of modern and classically trained dancers, and blending dance steps from ballet, modern, jazz, social dancing, and athletics. With the renewal of classical dance, practised more and more in France, the continuing investigations of modern dance, and all the new forms of expression in the US (jazz dance, tap dance, rock, break dancing), the 20th century could well be called the century of dance.

Rudolf Nureyev and Carolyn Carlson.

Le Sacre du Printemps, ballet by Maurice Béjart, 1986.

BALLET TERMS IN FRENCH AND ENGLISH

Adage [ah-dahzh′] (**or** *adagio*): **Adage** is French for the Italian word *adagio*, meaning "gently" or "at ease." It refers (1) to a series of exercises or movements performed to slow music; or (2) to the slow section of a *pas de deux*.

Arabesque [ah-rah-besk′]. A long, graceful pose made by balancing on the supporting leg while extending the free leg behind.

Ballon [bah-lohn′]. Bounciness. A dancer who jumps easily and lightly is said to have *ballon*.

Barre [bahr]. A wooden bar affixed horizontally to the walls of the dance studio.

Battement [baht-mahn′]. Literally, beating. A beating action of the leg or foot.

Batterie [bah-tree′]. Literally, battery. The general term for all very fast steps in which the legs beat against each other in the air.

Bras [brah]. Arms, arms.

Choreographer. A person who creates a ballet.

Cinquième. [san-kyem′]. Fifth; fifth position.

Classical, classic. (1) Style of dance that obeys the rules defined by the *Académie royale de danse* founded by Louis XIV. (2) Term applied to ballets created in the second half of the 19th century—for example, *The Nutcracker, Swan Lake, Coppélia*—in which form, pattern, and movement are the primary considerations.

Corps de ballet [kor duh bah-lay′]. The main body of dancers of a ballet company, who usually dance together as a group.

Cou-de-pied [koo-dih-pee-ay′]. The part of the foot between the ankle and the base of the calf. *Sur le cou-de-pied* means on the *coup-de-pied*; the working foot is cupped around the supporting leg.

Couronne, en [ahn koo-rohn′]. In the shape of a crown.

Croisé [krwah-zay′]. Literally, crossed. A particular placing of the body or limb as seen from the audience.

Dedans, en [en dih-dahn′]. Literally, inward. In steps and exercises, *en dedans* indicates that the leg moves from the back of the body and circles to the front.

Dégagé [day-gah-zhay′]. (1) Literally, disengaged (freed), or a disengaging step. (2) A pointing of the fully arched foot to an open position to the air on the floor in any given direction.

Dehors, en [ahn duh-aur′]. Literally, outward. (1) In steps and exercises, *en dehors* means that the leg moves in a circular direction, starting at the front and moving towards the back of the body. (2) Refers to the position in which the legs and feet are turned out from the hip joints.

Demi-hauteur [d′mee-oh-tuhr′]. Literally, at half height. The position of the foot at midheight, with the leg at a 45 degree angle to the floor.

Demi-plié [d′mee-plee-ay′]. Literally, half-bend. A movement in which the knees are bent only halfway, heels staying on the floor.

Demi-pointe [d′mee-pwant′]. On the balls of the feet: standing on the front part of the foot, arches and heels raised off the floor. Could be done on one foot or two.

Derrière [dih-ree-air′]. Behind, in back. May refer to a movement, step, or the placement of an arm or leg in back of the body. For steps, *derrière* means the working foot closes at the back.

Descendant, en [ahn dih-sahn-dahn′]. Advancing from the back of the stage to the front.

Devant [dih-vahn′]. In front.

Dos [doh]. The back of the body.

Ecart, grand [grahn tay-kar′]. The split.

Enchaînement [ahn-shain-mahn′]. A series of steps danced to a musical phrase; a combination.

Entrechat [ahn-trih-shah′]. Literally, interweaving. A step in which the dancer jumps straight up and crosses the legs in the air, a certain number of times.

Fondu, en [ahn fohn-diu′]. Literally, sinking down, melting. Has several meanings including (1) descent from a jump or *relevé* into a *plié*; (2) a lowering of the body made by bending the supporting leg at the knee.

Frappé [frah-pay′]. Striking.

Genou [zhnoo]. Knee. *Au genou* means "at or to the knee."

Glissade [glee-sahd]. A smooth traveling step that glides along the ground.

Grand, grande [grahn, grahnd]. Big, large, wide, deep.

Grand plié [grahn plee-ay′]. A complete bending of the legs until the thighs are in a horizontal position. The body remains upright and the back straight.

Haut, en [ahn-noh′]. high. A high position of the legs or arms.

Hauteur [oh-tuhr′]. Height. The leg is *à la hauteur* when it is raised at a right angle (or 90 degrees) to the body.

Jambe [zhahnb]. Leg.

Jeté [zheh-tay′]. Literally, throwing step. A jump from one foot to the other, done with a throwing movement of the leg.

Main [man]. Hand.

On point (*sur les pointes*). Dancing on the tips of the toes, which is done with the help of toe shoes.

Pas [pah]. Literally, step. (1) A simple step in any direction. (2) A simple or more complicated movement that transfers the weight of the body. (3) A dance by one or more persons.

Petit, petite [p'tee; p'teet]. Small, little.

Petits battements sur le cou-de-pied [p'tee baht-mahn' siur lih koo-di-pee-ay']. Literally, small beatings on the *cou-de-pied*. The working foot brushes in and out from front to back and back to front around the ankle of the supporting leg. Also called *petits battements serrés*.

Pied [pee-ay']. Foot.

Placé [plah-say']. Literally, placed. A term used to indicate that the dancer's *aplomb*, or alignment, is correct.

Plié [plee-ay']. Bend. See *Demi-plié* or *Grand plié*.

Pointé [pwan-tay']. Pointed.

Pointes, sur les [siur lay pwant']. On the points or tips of the toes; point work.

Port de bras. [por dih brah']. Literally, the carriage of the arms. (1) Any movement of the arms in ballet. (2) Exercises of the arms to make them move more harmoniously.

Positions of the feet. In classic French dance, there are five basic positions of the feet.

Première [prehm-yair']. First; first position.

Quatrième [kah-tree-ehm']. Fourth; fourth position.

Quatrième derrière [kah-tree-ehm' dih-ree-air']. Position in which the working leg is taken to the back to create a fourth position. If the foot is raised it is *grand quatrième derrière*.

Quatrième devant [kah-tree-em dih-vahn']. Position in which the working leg moves to the front to create fourth position.

Raccourci [rah-koor-see']. See *Retiré*.

Relevé [rih-leh-vay']. Literally, relifted. Movement consisting of raising the body up on *demi-pointe* or *pointe*; or it may refer to lowering the heel of the working foot from a *tendu pointé* position and reraising it to the same position.

Remontant, en [ahn rih-mohn-tahn']. Indicates that the working leg moves from the front to the back, thus the dancer moves from the front of the stage backwards.

Retiré [rih-tih-ray']. Literally, withdrawn. A movement in which the thigh of the working leg is raised to second position in the air (*en l'air*) so that the toe touches the knee of the supporting leg either in front or in back. Also called *raccourci*.

Rond de jambe [rohn dih zhahnb']. Literally, a circle made by the leg. The dancer stands on one leg, while the free leg is extended and describes a half circle. It may be done in the air or on the ground.

Saut [soh]. A jump.

Seconde [seh-gohnd']. Second; second position.

Soubresaut [soo-brih-soh']. A vertical jump, done while keeping both legs well extended and the feet together.

Supporting leg. The leg that supports the body's weight; the standing leg.

Sur [siur]. On, upon.

Tendu, tendue [tahn-diu']. Stretched.

Terre, à [ah tair']. On the ground.

Troisième [trwah-zyem']. Third; third position.

Turnout. One of the basic principles of classical dance; due to the working of the joints (hips, knees, ankles), the legs are turned outward.

Variation [vah-ree-ah-syon']. Any solo dance in a classical ballet, usually a series of difficult movements.

Working leg. The leg that moves.

INDEX

INDEX